Nicholas Barnaud Delphinas
The Book of Lambspring

The Book of Lambspring,
A Noble Ancient Philosopher,
Concerning the Philosophical Stone;
Rendered into Latin Verse by
Nicholas Barnaud Delphinas,
Doctor of Medicine, a zealous Student of this Art.

PREFACE

I am called Lambspring, born of a Noble Family, and
this Crest I bear
with Glory and Justice.

Philosophy I have read, and thoroughly understood,
The utmost depth of my teachers' knowledge have I
sounded.
This God graciously granted to me,
Giving me a heart to understand wisdom.
Thus I became the Author of this Book,
And I have clearly set forth the whole matter,
That Rich and Poor might understand.

There is nothing like it upon earth;
Nor (God be praised) have I therein forgotten my
humble self.
I am acquainted with the only true foundation:
Therefore preserve this Book with care,
And take heed that you study it again and again.
Thus shall you receive and learn the truth,
And use this great gift of God for good ends.
O God the Father, which art of all the beginning and
end,
We beseech thee for the sake of our Lord Jesus Christ
To enlighten our minds and thoughts,
That we may praise Thee without ceasing,
And accomplish this Book according to Thy will!
Direct Thou everything to a good end,
And preserve us through Thy great mercy. -
With the help of God I will shew you this Art,
And will not hide or veil the truth from you.
After that you understand me aright,
You will soon be free from the bonds of error.
For there is only one substance,
In which all the rest is hidden;
Therefore, keep a good heart.
Coction, time, and patience are what you need;
If you would enjoy the precious reward,
You must cheerfully give both time and labour.
For you must subject to gentle coction the seeds and the
metals,
Day by day, during several weeks;
Thus in this one vile thing
You will discover and bring to perfection the whole

work of Philosophy,
Which to most men appears impossible,
Though it is a convenient and easy task.
If we were to shew it to the outer world
We should be derided by men, women, and children.
Therefore be modest and secret,
And you will be left in peace and security.
Remember your duty towards your neighbour and your
God,
Who gives this Art, and would have it concealed.
Now we will conclude the Preface,
That we may begin to describe the very Art,
And truly and plainly set it forth in figures,
Rendering thanks to the Creator of every creature.
Hereunto follows the First Figure,

Be warned and understand truly that two fishes are swimming in our sea.

The Sea is the Body, the two Fishes are Soul and Spirit.
The Sages will tell you
That two fishes are in our sea
Without any flesh or bones.
Let them be cooked in their own water;
Then they also will become a vast sea,
The vastness of which no man can describe.
Moreover, the Sages say
That the two fishes are only one, not two;
They are two, and nevertheless they are one,
Body, Spirit, and Soul.
Now, I tell you most truly,
Cook these three together,
That there may be a very large sea.
Cook the sulphur well with the sulphur,
And hold your tongue about it:
Conceal your knowledge to your own advantage,
And you shall be free from poverty.
Only let your discovery remain a close secret.

Here you straightway behold a black beast in the forest.

Putrefaction.
The Sage says
That a wild beast is in the forest,
Whose skin is of the blackest dye.
If any man cut off his head,
His blackness will disappear,
And give place to a snowy white.
Understand well the meaning of this head:
The blackness is called the head of the Raven;
As soon as it disappears,
A white colour is straightway manifested;
It is given this name, despoiled of its head.
When the Beast's black hue has vanished in a black
smoke,
The Sages rejoice
From the bottom of their hearts;
But they keep it a close secret,
That no foolish man may know it.
Yet unto their Sons, in kindness of heart,
They partly reveal it in their writings;
And therefore let those who receive the gift
Enjoy it also in silence,
Since God would have it concealed.

Hear without terror that in the forest are hidden a deer
and an unicorn.

In the Body there is Soul and Spirit.
The Sages say truly
That two animals are in this forest:
One glorious, beautiful, and swift,
A great and strong deer;
The other an unicorn.
They are concealed in the forest,
But happy shall that man be called
Who shall snare and capture them.
The Masters shew you here clearly
That in all places
These two animals wander about in forests
(But know that the forest is but one).
If we apply the parable to our Art,
We shall call the forest the Body.
That will be rightly and truly said.
The unicorn will be the Spirit at all times.
The deer desires no other name
But that of the Soul; which name no man shall take
away from it.
He that knows how to tame and master them by Art,
To couple them together,
And to lead them in and out of the forest,
May justly be called a Master.
For we rightly judge
That he has attained the golden flesh,
And may triumph everywhere;
Nay, he may bear rule over great Augustus.

Here you behold a great marvel --- two lions are joined into one.

The Spirit and Soul must be united in their Body.
The Sages do faithfully teach us
That two strong lions, to wit, male and female,
Lurk in a dark and rugged valley.
These the Master must catch,
Though they are swift and fierce,
And of terrible and savage aspect.
He who, by wisdom and cunning,
Can snare and bind them,
And lead them into the same forest,
Of him it may be said with justice and truth
That he has merited the meed of praise before all others,
And that his wisdom transcends that of the worldly
wise.

A wolf and a dog are in one house, and are afterwards changed into one.

The Body is mortified and rendered white, then joined
to Soul and Spirit by being saturated with them.
Alexander writes from Persia
That a wolf and a dog are in this field,
Which, as the Sages say,
Are descended from the same stock,
But the wolf comes from the east,
And the dog from the west.
They are full of jealousy,
Fury, rage, and madness;
One kills the other,
And from them comes a great poison.
But when they are restored to life,
They are clearly shewn to be
The Great and Precious Medicine,
The most glorious Remedy upon earth,
Which refreshes and restores the Sages,
Who render thanks to God, and do praise Him.

This surely is a great miracle and without any deception - that in a venomous dragon there should be the great medicine.

The Mercury is precipitated or sublimed, dissolved in its
own proper water,
and then once more coagulated.
A savage Dragon lives in the forest,
Most venomous he is, yet lacking nothing:
When he sees the rays of the Sun and its bright fire,
He scatters abroad his poison,
And flies upward so fiercely
That no living creature can stand before him,
Nor is even the Basilisk equal to him.
He who hath skill to slay him, wisely
Hath escaped from all dangers.
Yet all venom, and colours, are multiplied
In the hour of his death.
His venom becomes the great Medicine.
He quickly consumes his venom,
For he devours his poisonous tail.
All this is performed on his own body,
From which flows forth glorious Balm,
With all its miraculous virtues.
Hereat all the Sages do loudly rejoice.

We hear two birds in the forest, yet we must understand them to be only one.

The Mercury having been often sublimed, is at length
fixed, and becomes capable of resisting fire: the
sublimation must be repeated until at length the fixation
is attained.
A nest is found in the forest,
In which Hermes has his brood;
One fledgling always strives to fly upward,
The other rejoices to sit quietly in the nest;
Yet neither can get away from the other.
The one that is below holds the one that is above,
And will not let it get away from the nest,
As a husband in a house with his wife,
Bound together in closest bonds of wedlock.
So also do we rejoice at all times,
That we hold the female eagle fast in this way,
And we render thanks to God the Father.

Here are two birds, great and strong - the body and spirit; one devours the other.

Let the Body be placed in horse-dung, or a warm bath, the Spirit having been extracted from it. The Body has become white by the process, the Spirit red by our Art. All that exists tends towards perfection, and thus is the Philosopher's Stone prepared.

In India there is a most pleasant wood,
In which two birds are bound together.
One is of a snowy white; the other is red.
They bite each other, and one is slain
And devoured by the other.
Then both are changed into white doves,
And of the Dove is born a Phoenix,
Which has left behind blackness and foul death,
And has regained a more glorious life.
This power was given it by God Himself,
That it might live eternally, and never die.
It gives us wealth, it preserves our life,
And with it we may work great miracles,
As also the true Philosophers do plainly inform us.

The lord of the forests has recovered his kingdom, and mounted from the lowest to the highest degree. If fortune smile, you may from a rhetor become a consul; if fortune frown, the consul may become a rhetor.

Thus you may know that the Tincture has truly attained
the first degree.
Now hear of a wonderful deed,
For I will teach you great things,
How the King rises high above all his race;
And hear also what the noble lord of the forest says:
I have overcome and vanquished my foes,
I have trodden the venomous Dragon under foot,
I am a great and glorious King in the earth.
There is none greater than I,
Child either of the Artist or of Nature,
Among all living creatures.
I do all that man can desire,
I give power and lasting health,
Also gold, silver, gems, and precious stones,
And the panacea for great and small diseases.
Yet at first I was of ignoble birth,
Till I was set in a high place.
To reach this lofty summit
Was given me by God and Nature.
Thence from the meanest I became the highest,
And mounted to the most glorious throne,
And to the state of royal sovereignty:
Therefore Hermes has called me the Lord of the
Forests.

A salamander lives in the fire, which imparts to it a most glorious hue.

This is the reiteration, gradation, and ameliorationof the
Tincture, or Philosopher's Stone; and the whole is called
its Augmentation.
In all fables we are told
That the Salamander is born in the fire;
In the fire it has that food and life
Which Nature herself has assigned to it.
It dwells in a great mountain
Which is encompassed by many flames,
And one of these is ever smaller than another -
Herein the Salamander bathes.
The third is greater, the fourth brighter than the rest -
In all these the Salamander washes, and is purified.
Then he hies him to his cave,
But on the way is caught and pierced
So that it dies, and yields up its life with its blood.
But this, too, happens for its good:
For from its blood it wins immortal life,
And then death has no more power over it.
Its blood is the most precious Medicine upon earth,
The same has not its like in the world.
For this blood drives away all disease
In the bodies of metals,
Of men, and of beasts.
From it the Sages derive their science,
And through it they attain the Heavenly Gift,
Which is called the Philosopher's Stone,
Possessing the power of the whole world.
This gift the Sages impart to us with loving hearts,
That we may remember them for ever.

The father and the son have linked their hands with
those of the guide: know that the three are body, soul,
and spirit.
Here is an old father of Israel,
Who has an only Son,
A Son whom he loves with all his heart.
With sorrow he prescribes sorrow to him.
He commits him to a guide,
Who is to conduct him whithersoever he will.
The Guide addresses the Son in these words:
Come hither! I will conduct thee everywhere,
To the summit of the loftiest mountain,
That thou mayest understand all wisdom,
That thou mayest behold the greatness of the earth, and
of the sea,
And then derive true pleasure.
I will bear thee through the air
To the gates of highest heaven.
The Son hearkened to the words of the Guide,
And ascended upward with him;
There saw he the heavenly throne,
That was beyond measure glorious.
When he had beheld these things,
He remembered his Father with sighing,
Pitied the great sorrow of his Father,
And said: I will return to his breast.

Another mountain of India lies in the vessel, which the
spirit and the soul - that is, the son and the guide - have
climbed.

Says the Son to the Guide:
I will go down to my Father,
For he cannot live without me.
He sighs and calls aloud for me.
And the Guide makes answer to the Son:
I will not let thee go alone;
From thy Father's bosom I brought thee forth,
I will also take thee back again,
That he may rejoice again and live.
This strength will we give unto him.
So both arose without delay,
And returned to the Father's house.
When the Father saw his Son coming,
He cried aloud, and said: -

Here the father devours the son; the soul and spirit flow
forth from the body.
My Son, I was dead without thee,
And lived in great danger of my life.
I revive at thy return,
And it fills my breast with joy.
But when the Son entered the Father's house,
The Father took him to his heart,
And swallowed him out of excessive joy,
And that with his own mouth.
The great exertion makes the Father sweat.

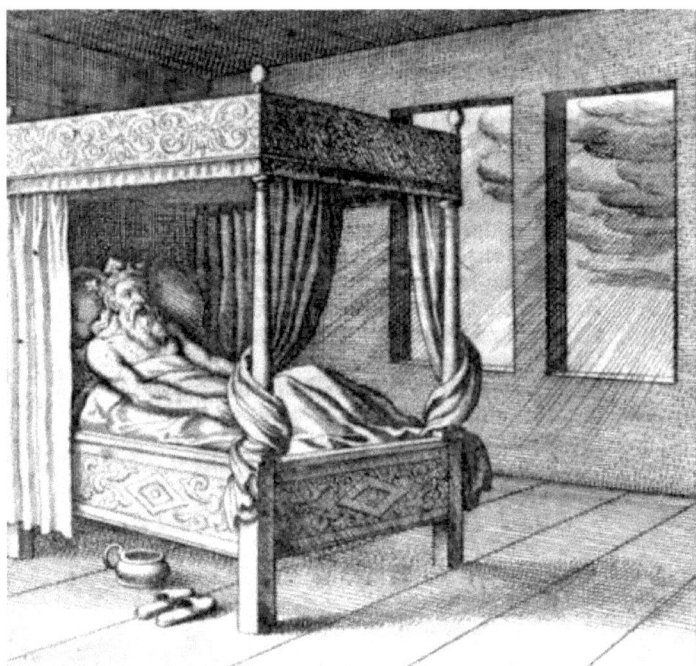

Here the father sweats profusely, while oil and the true
tincture of the sages flow forth from him.
Here the Father sweats on account of the Son,
And earnestly beseeches God,
Who has created everything in His hands,
Who creates, and has created all things,
To bring forth his Son from his body,
And to restore him to his former life.
God hearkens to his prayers,
And bids the Father lie down and sleep.
Then God sends down rain from heaven
To the earth from the shining stars.
It was a fertilizing, silver rain,
Which bedewed and softened the Father's Body.
Succour us, Lord, at the end,
That we may obtain Thy gracious Gift!

Here father and son are joined in one so to remain for
ever.
The sleeping Father is here changed
Entirely into limpid water,
And by virtue of this water alone
The good work is accomplished.
There is now a glorified and beautiful Father,
And he brings forth a new Son.
The Son ever remains in the Father,
And the Father in the Son.
Thus in divers things
They produce untold, precious fruit.
They perish never more,
And laugh at death.
By the grace of God they abide for ever,
The Father and the Son, triumphing gloriously
In the splendour of their new Kingdom.
Upon one throne they sit,
And the face of the Ancient Master
Is straightway seen between them:
He is arrayed in a crimson robe.
To the invisible king of the world,
To the only true and immortal god
Be praise and glory
Now and evermore.
Amen.

www.ingramcontent.com/pod-product-compliance
Lightning Source LLC
Chambersburg PA
CBHW071752090426
42738CB00011B/2661